European Vacation Coloring Book
Volume 1

Relaxed Cat

Aquinicum Press

www.AquinicumPress.com

For additional information contact RelaxedCat@AquinicumPress.com

European Vacation Volume 1/ Relaxed Cat. -- 1st ed.

ISBN: 1519785496
ISBN-13: 978-1519785497

DEDICATION

To the felines and their humans of the second smallest continent.

This is an **unusual** coloring book.

I produced these illustrations while on a trip to Europe.

The main objective of the trip was to visit friends, but I made sketches of various sites as well. The pictures in this volume, for example, are from Lativa.

However, my time was not entirely my own - I had a schedule to keep, and so the pictures are all unfinished in various degrees.

I've therefore provided you with this copy so that we can collaborate on completing them in a co-creation process.

How you proceed is entirely up to you - I'm going to be happy with the results. Many coloring possibilities are available. One can simply shade in a few parts to liven up the drawings with color, complete the images with a pen before coloring the figures and buildings, or engage in a detailed treatment of each visual element, with perhaps the occasional accent in metallic pen.

The key, however, is ensuring that the process is fun and relaxing - I'm confident it will be.

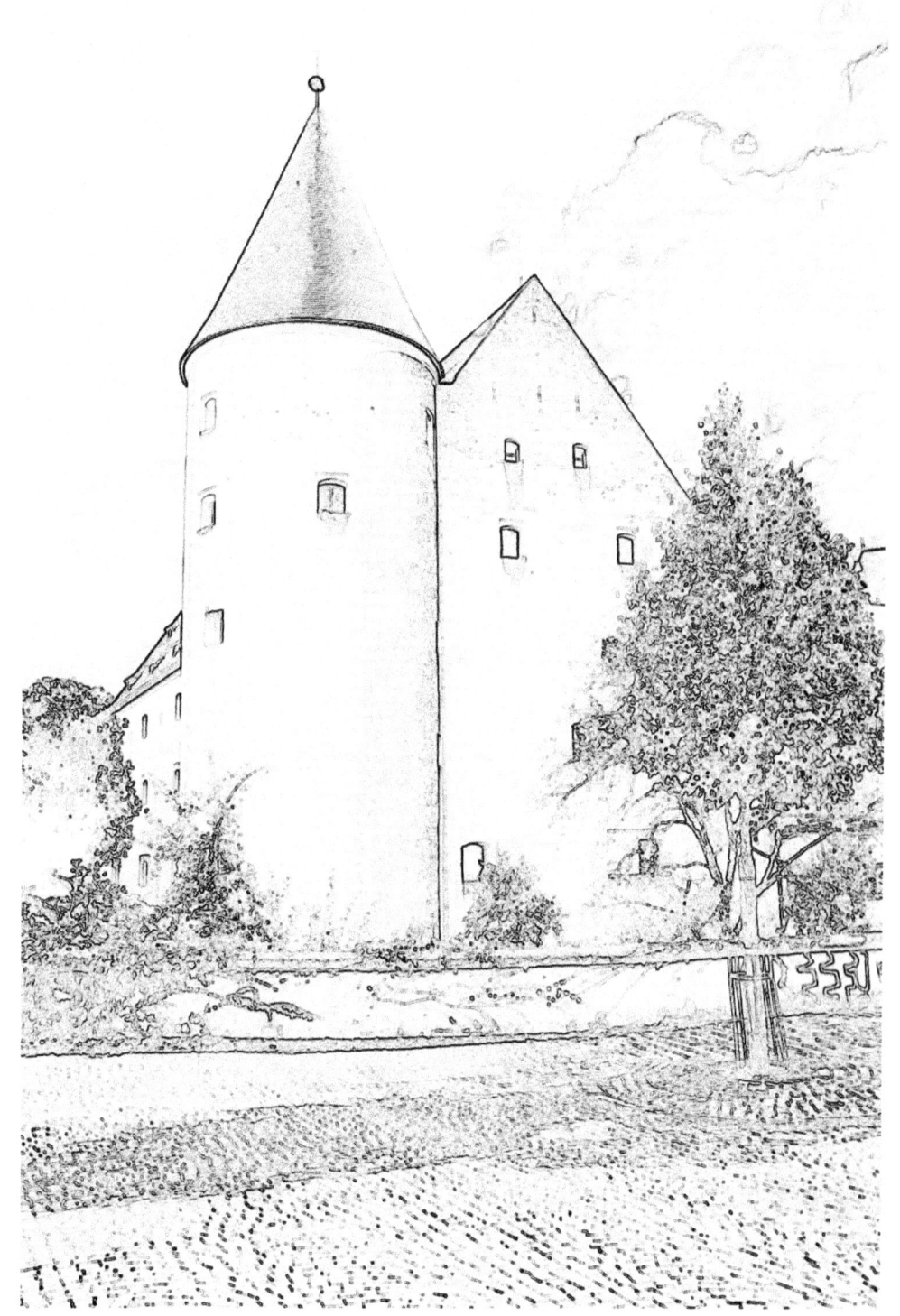

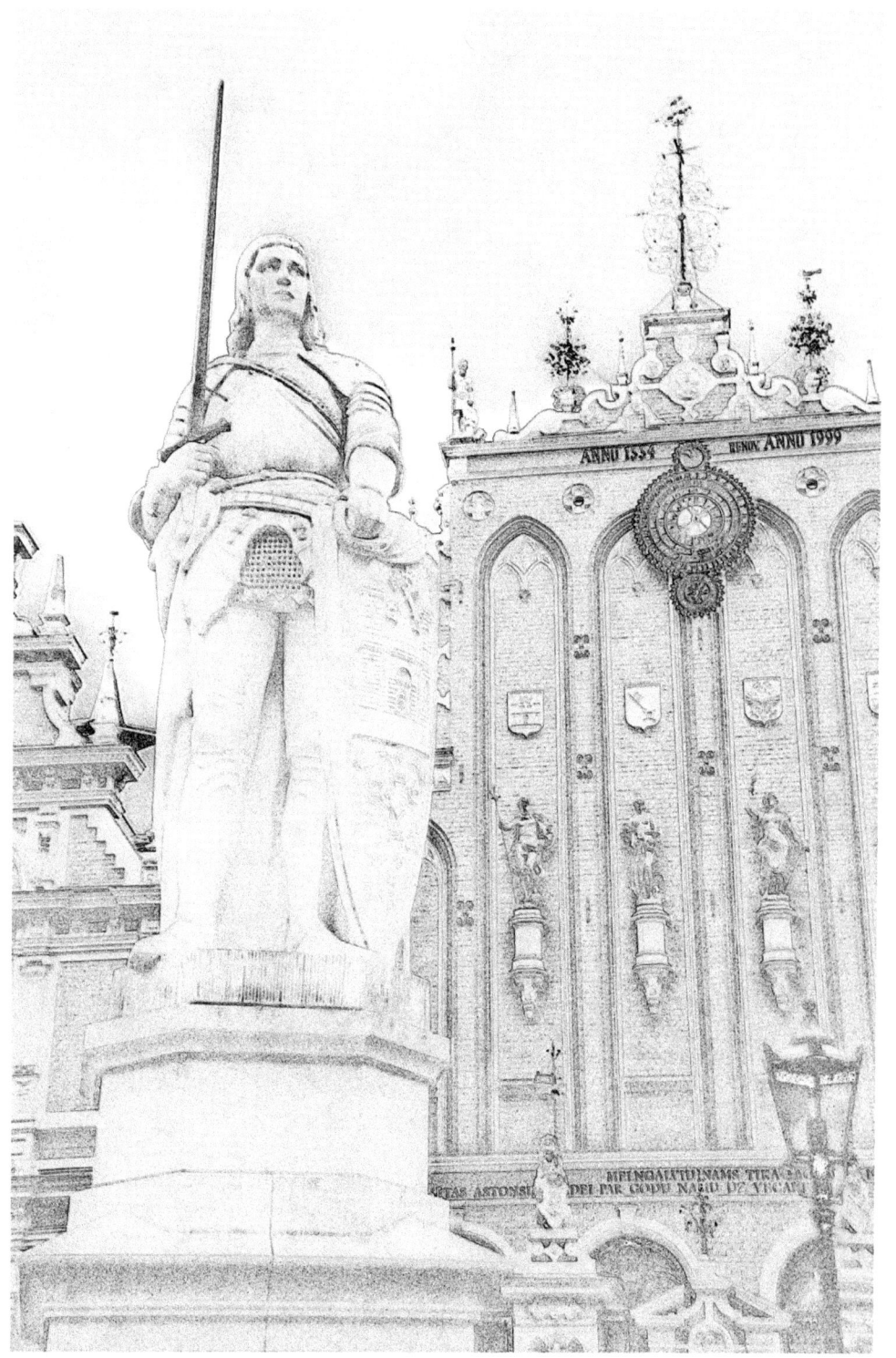

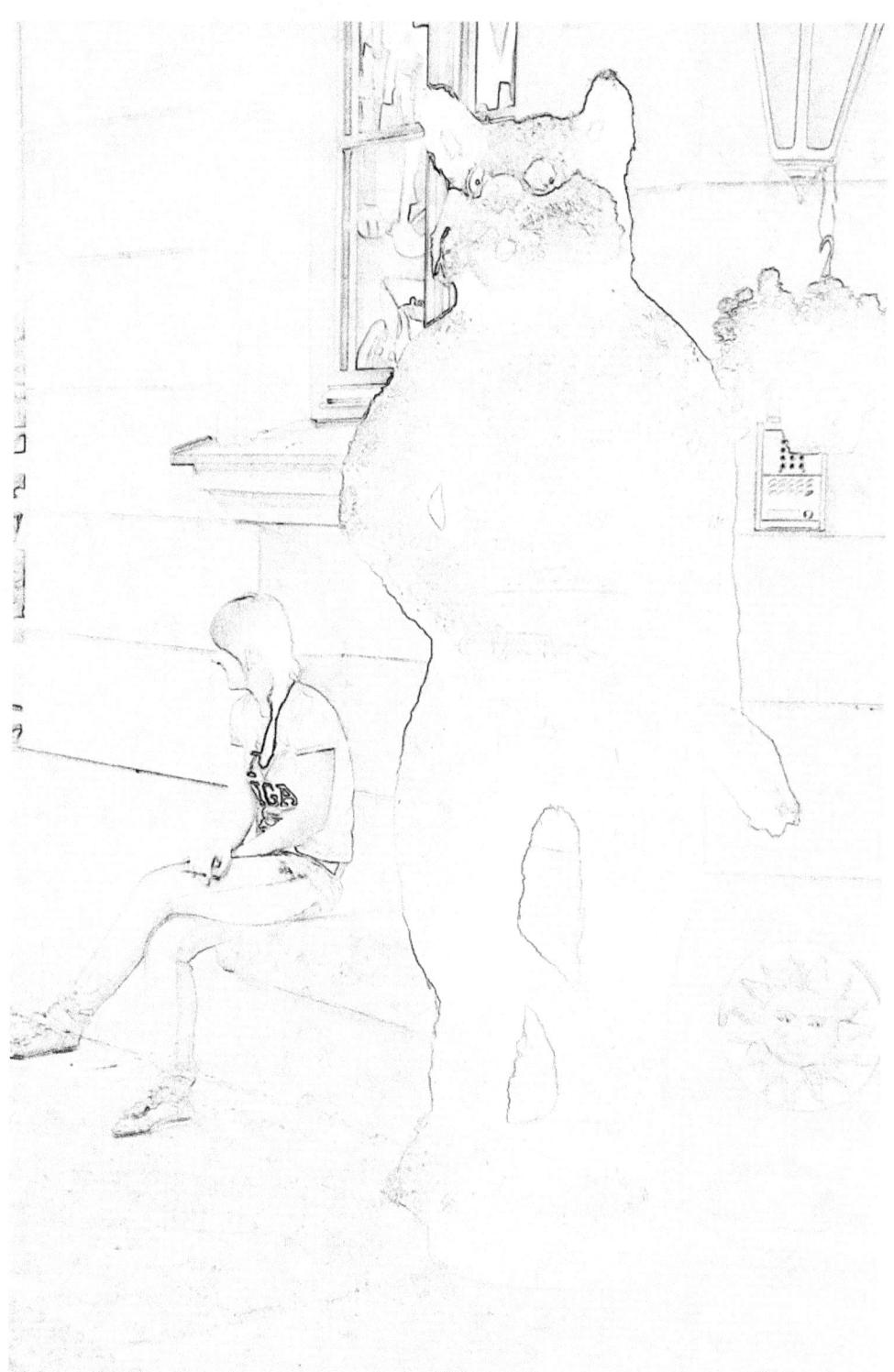

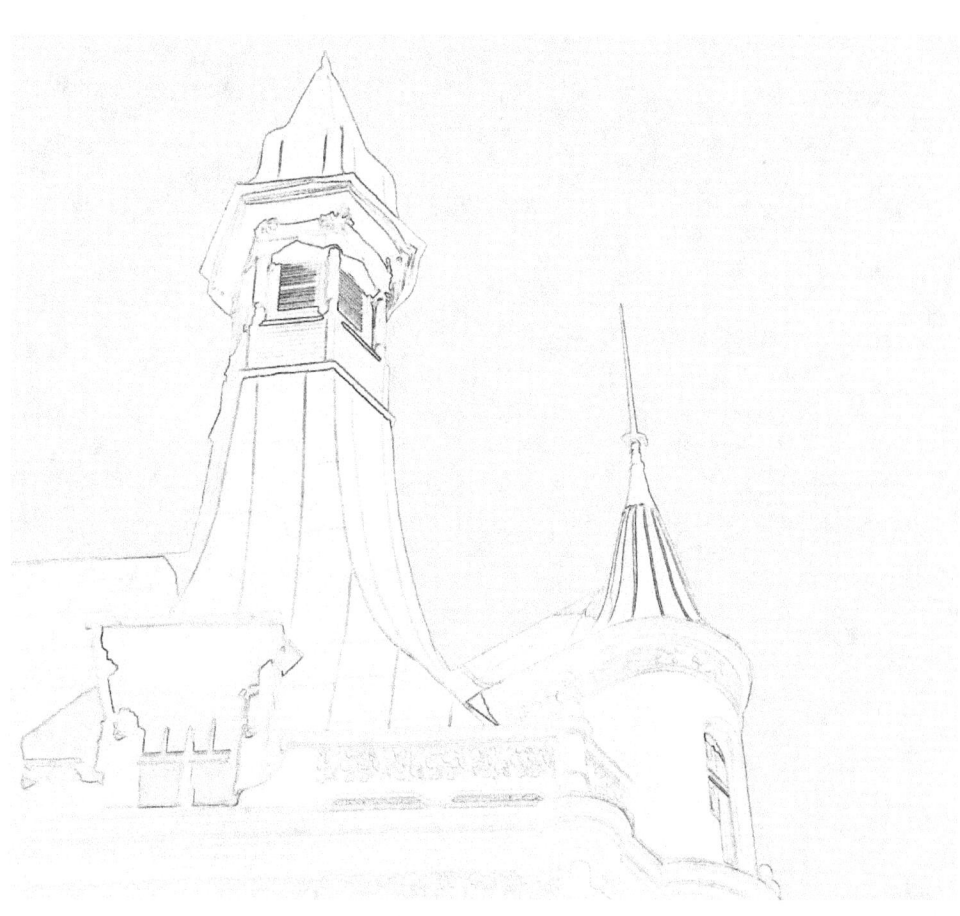

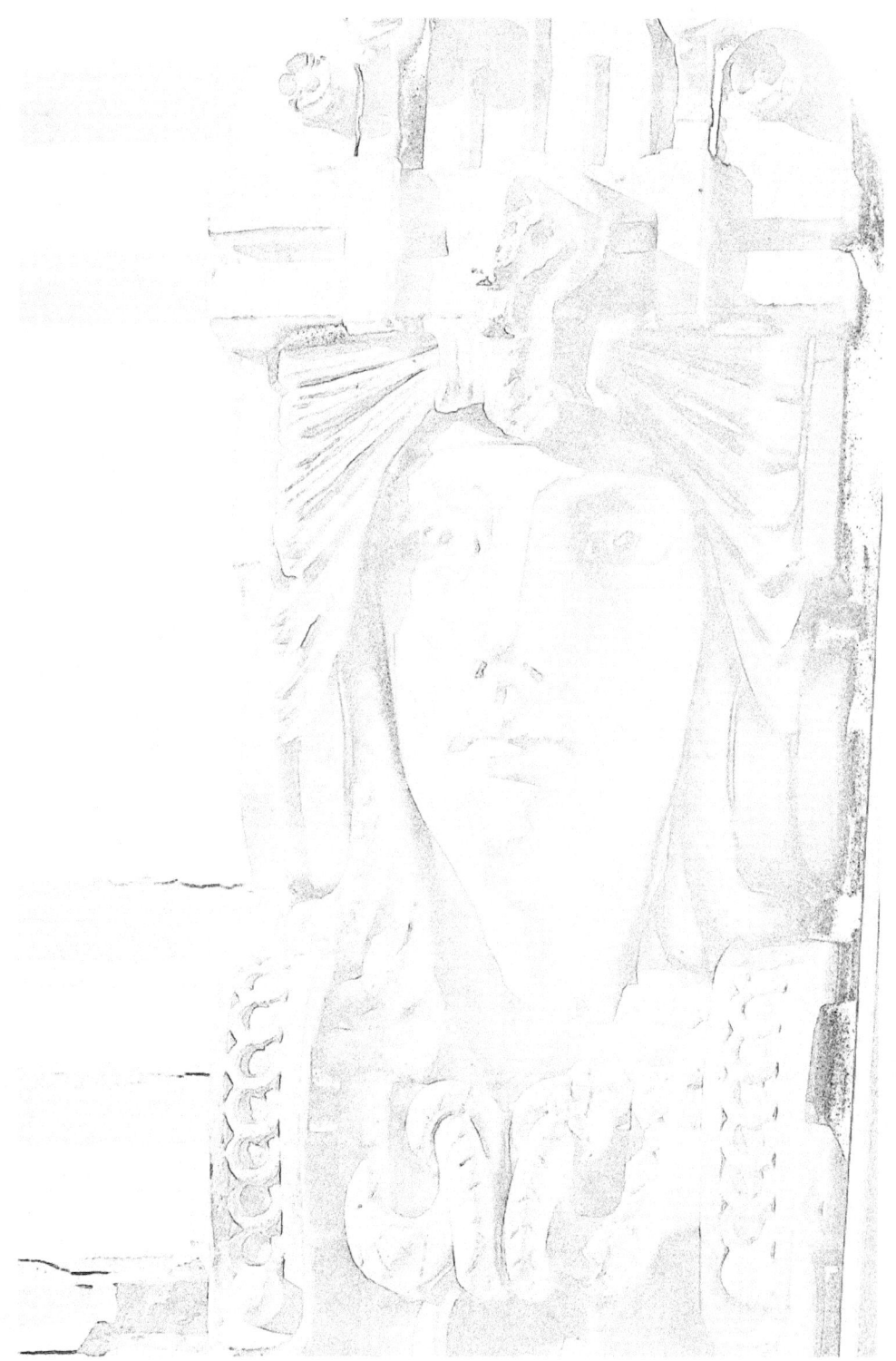

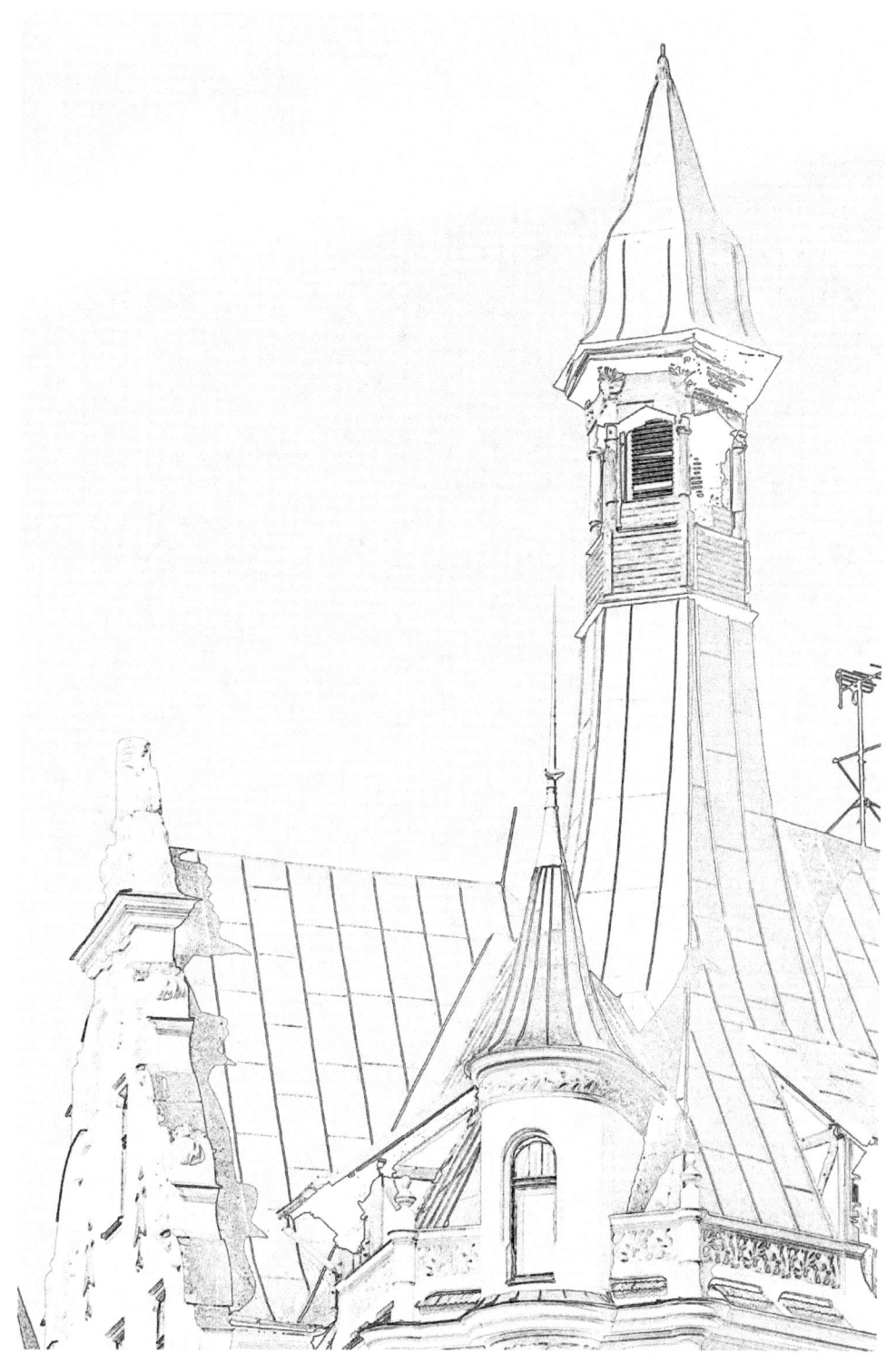

13

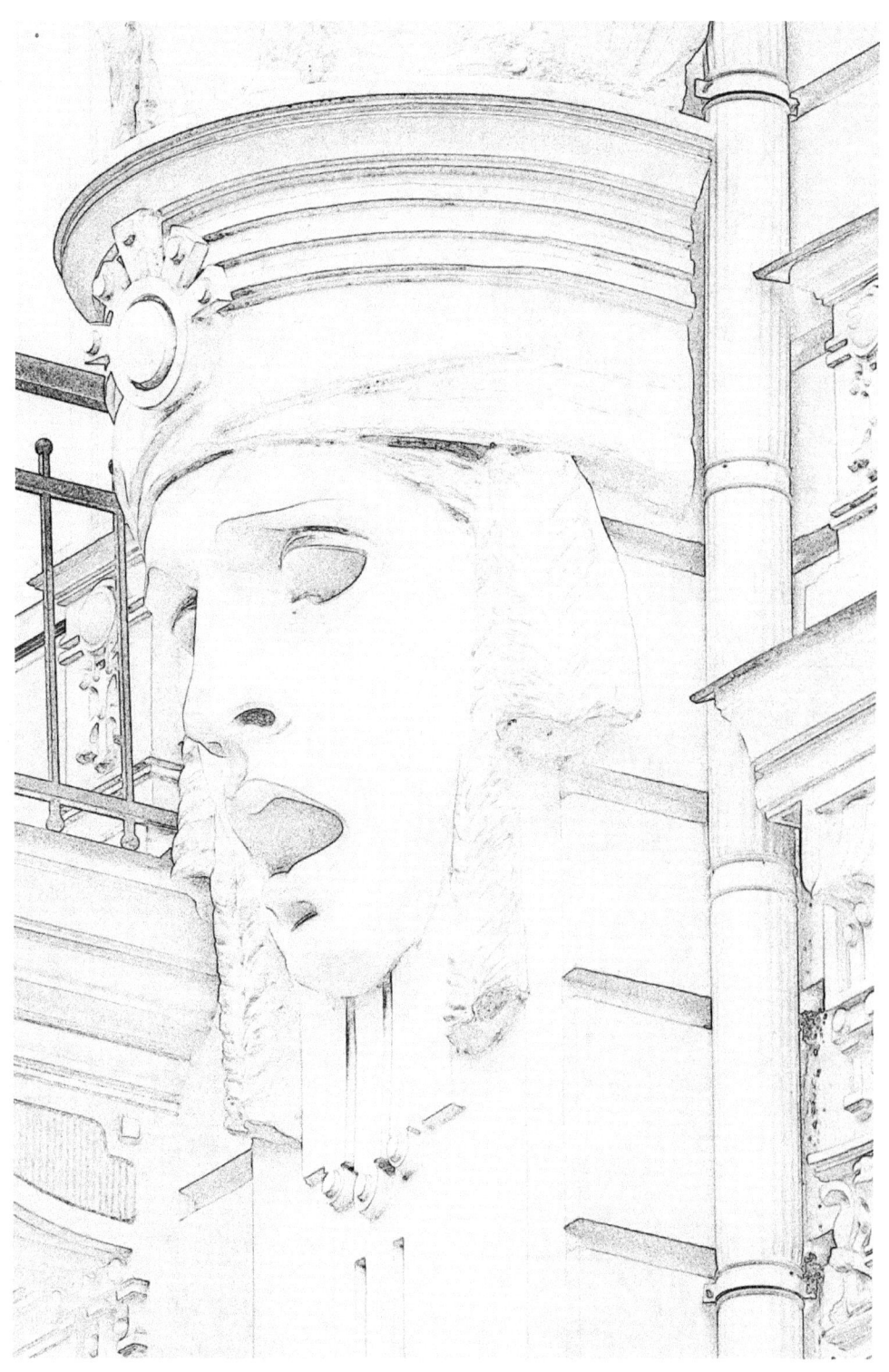

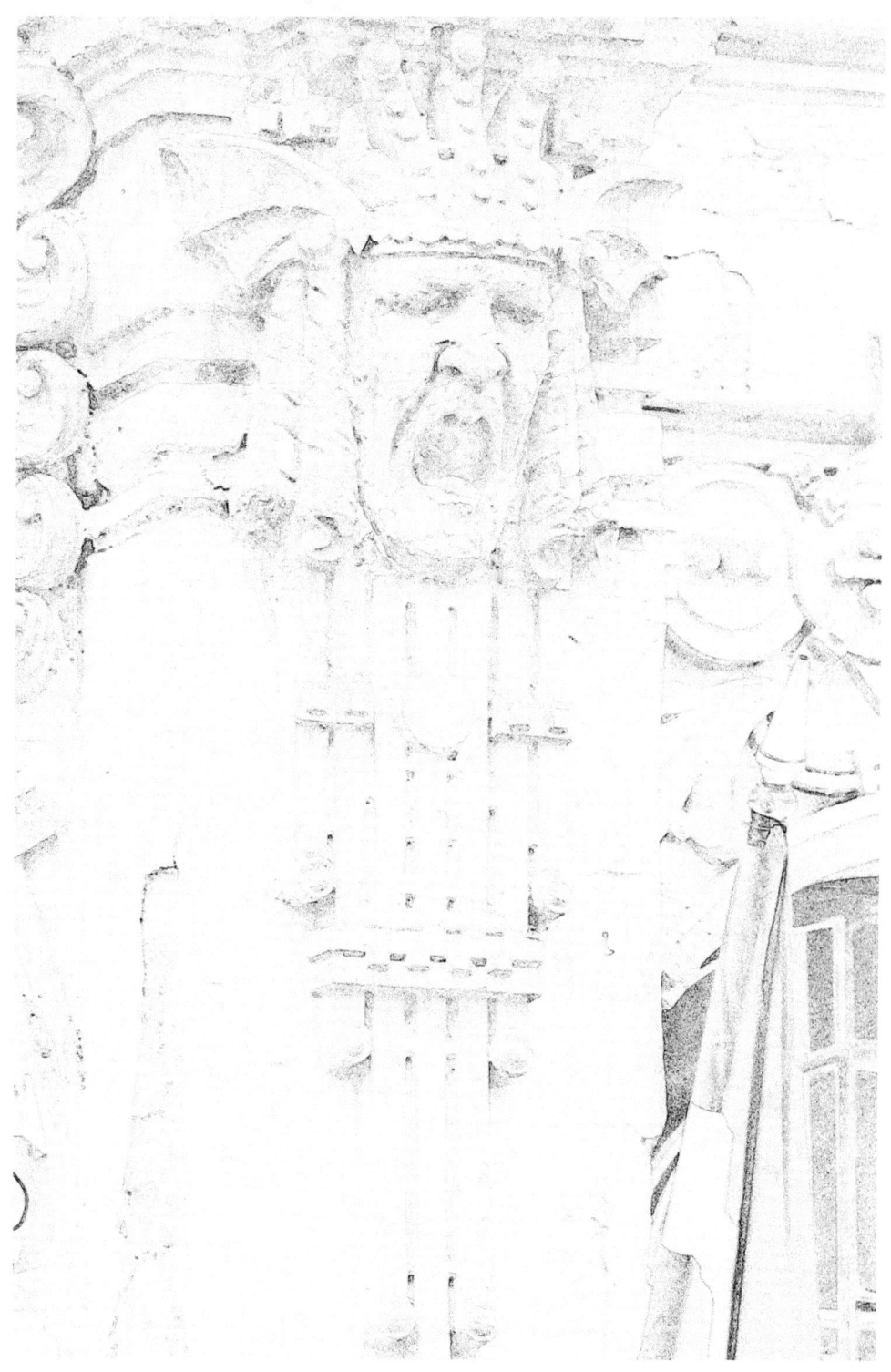

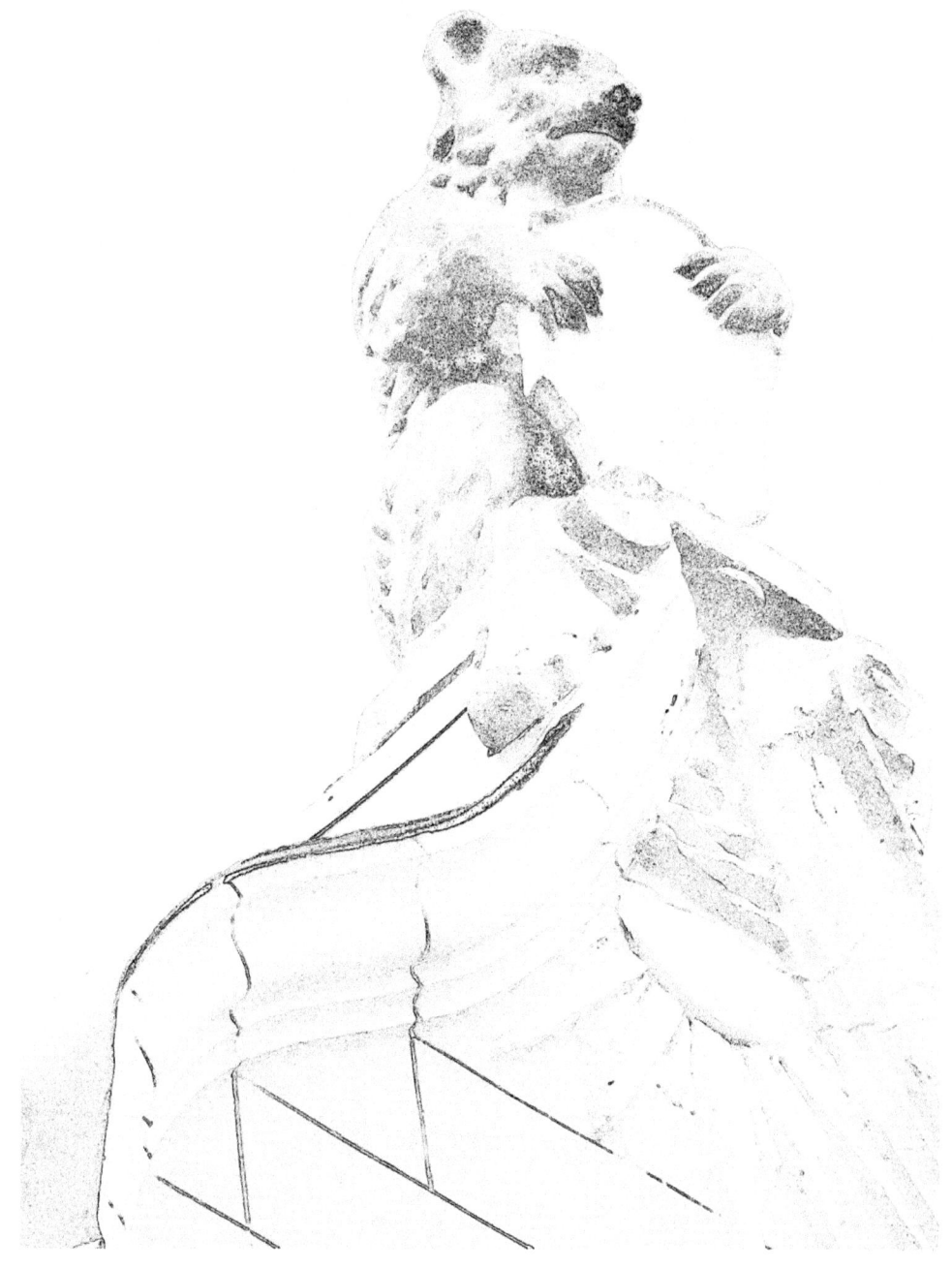

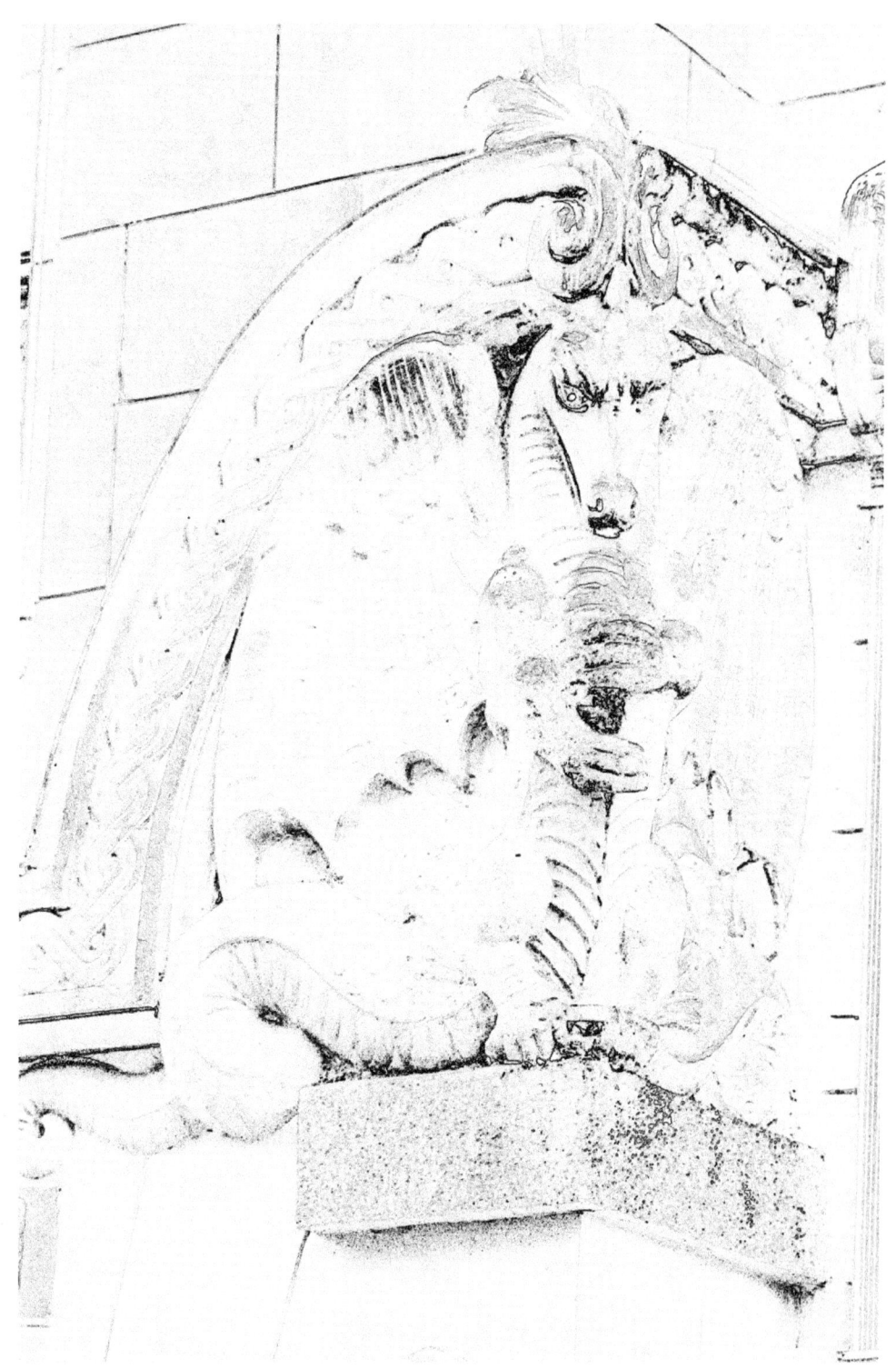

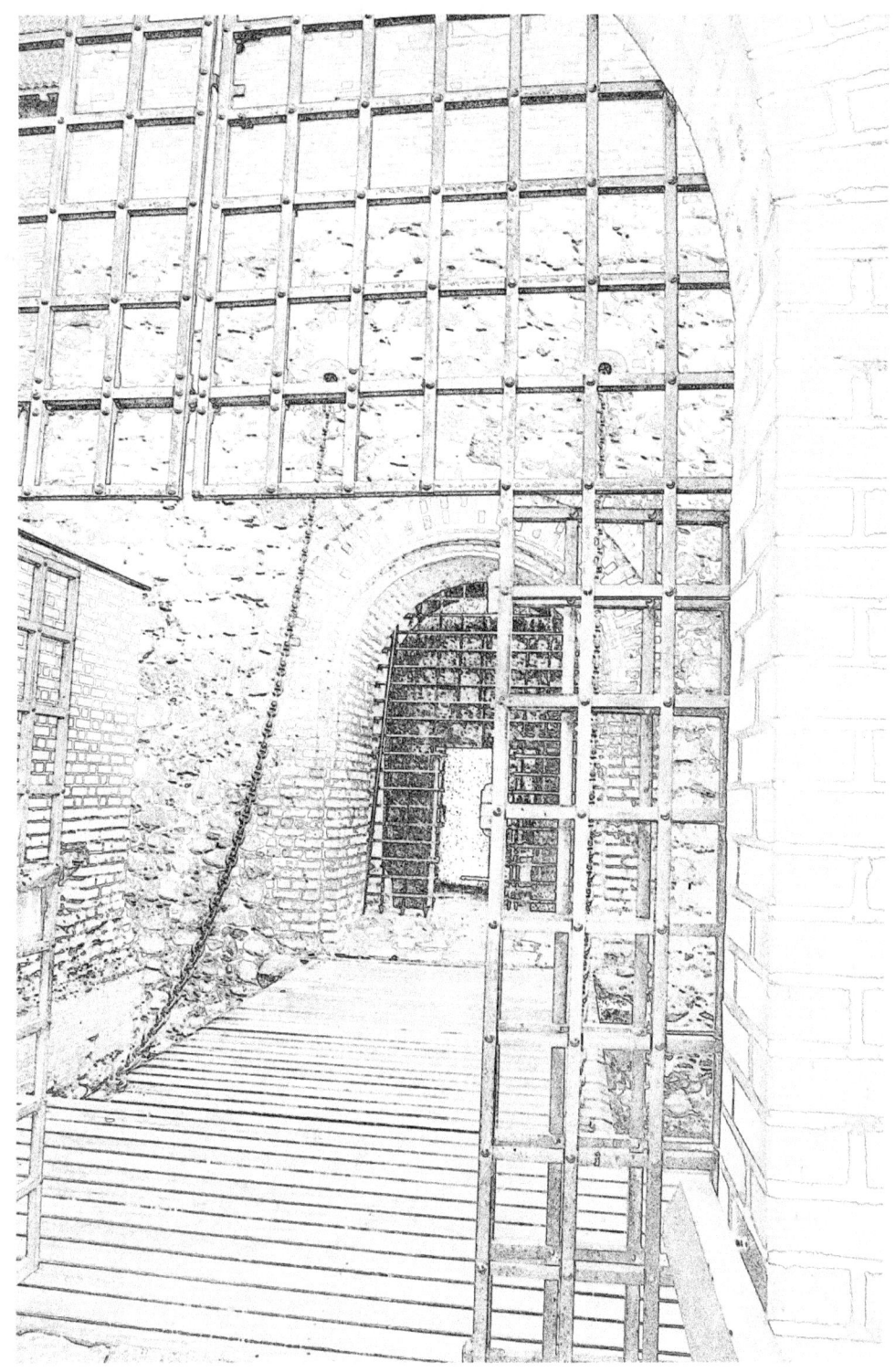

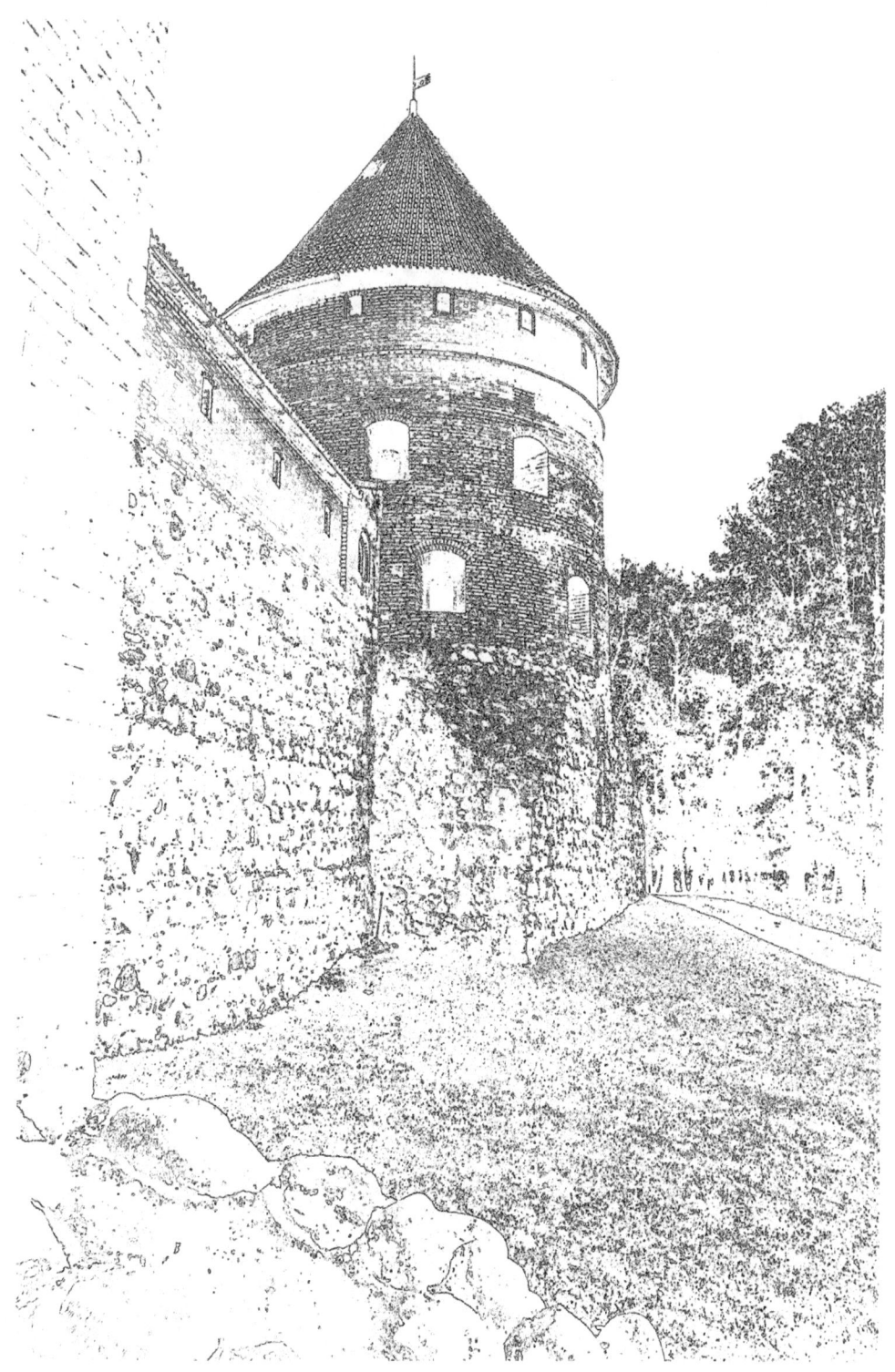

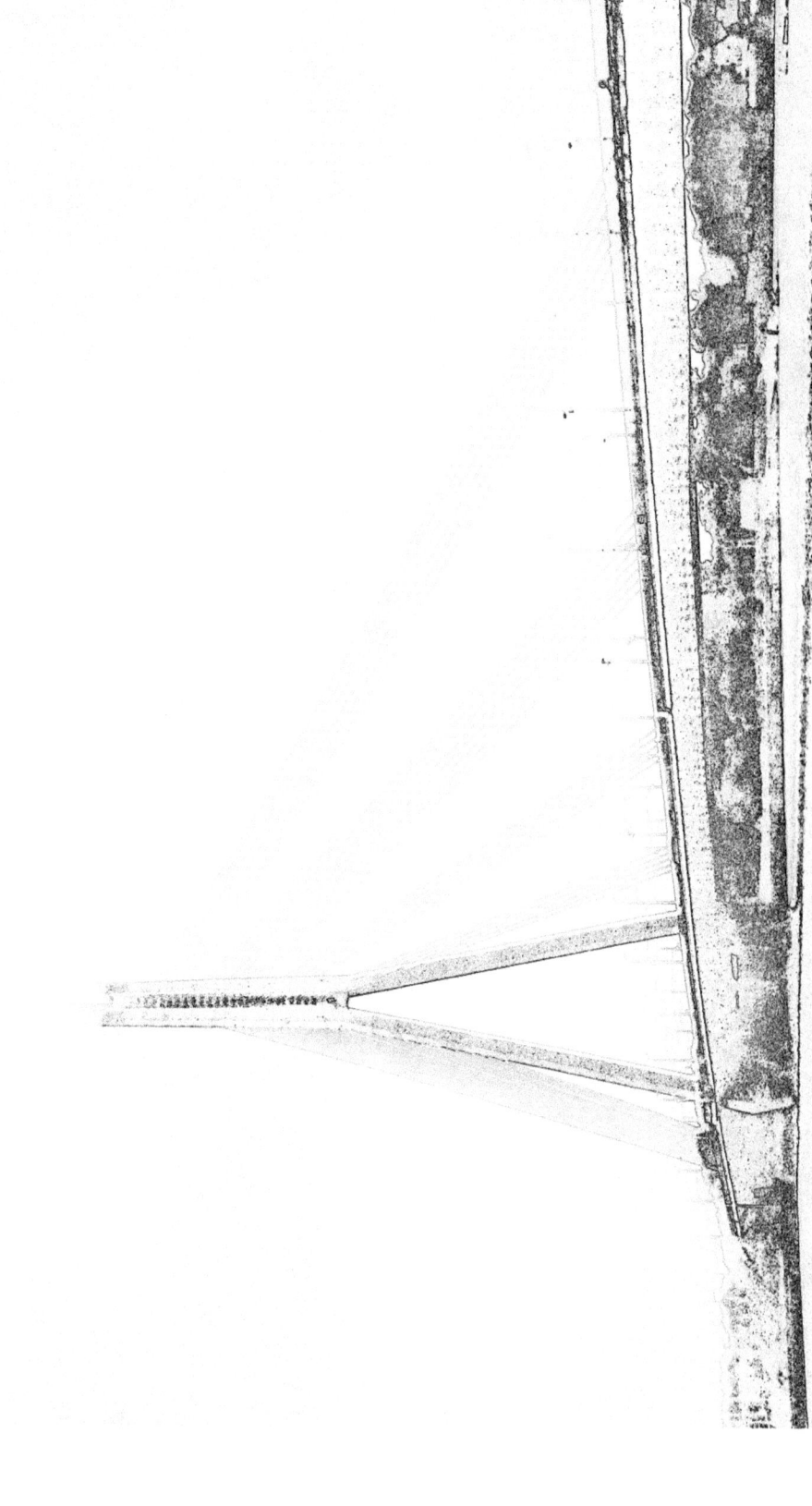

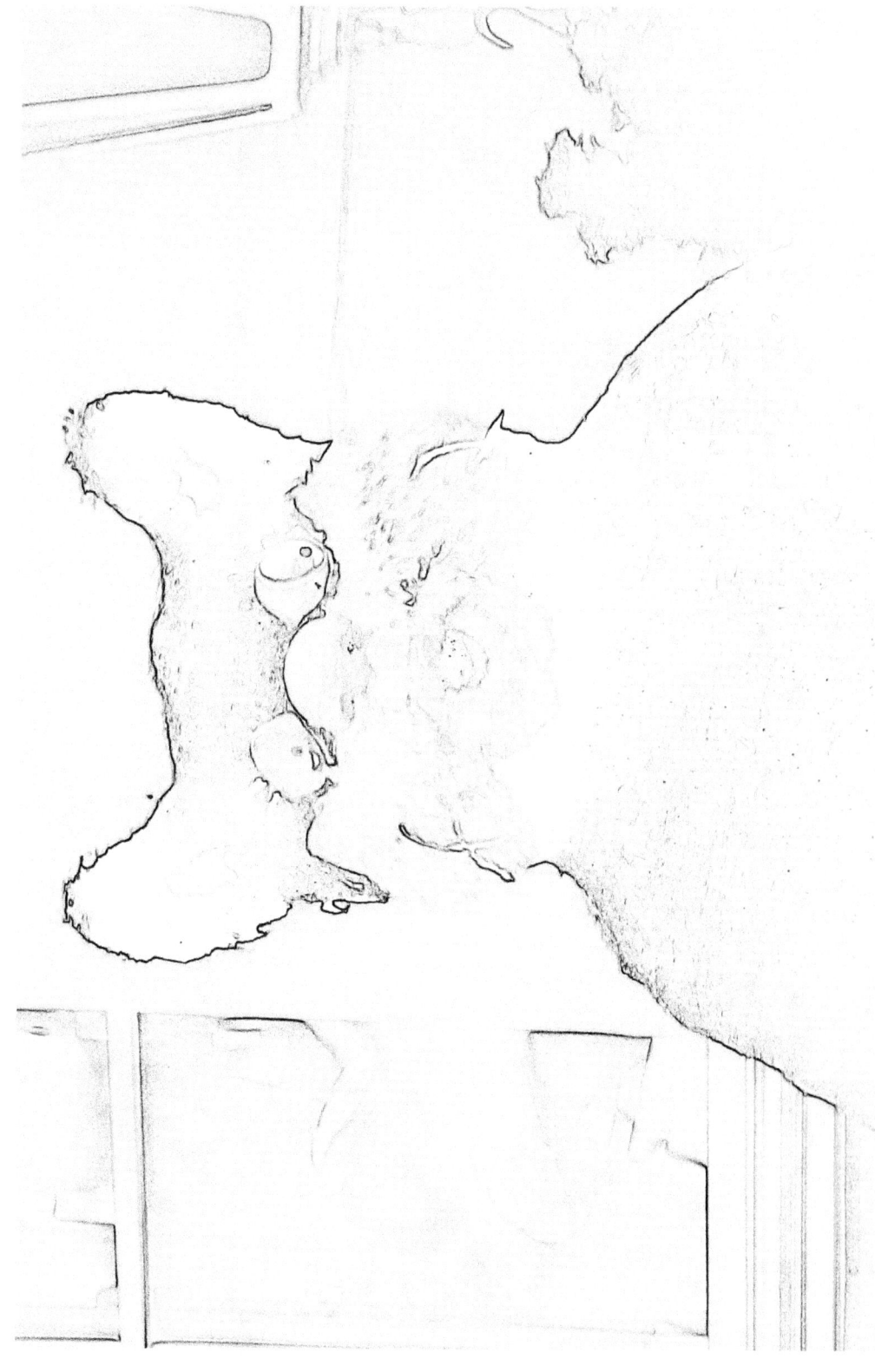

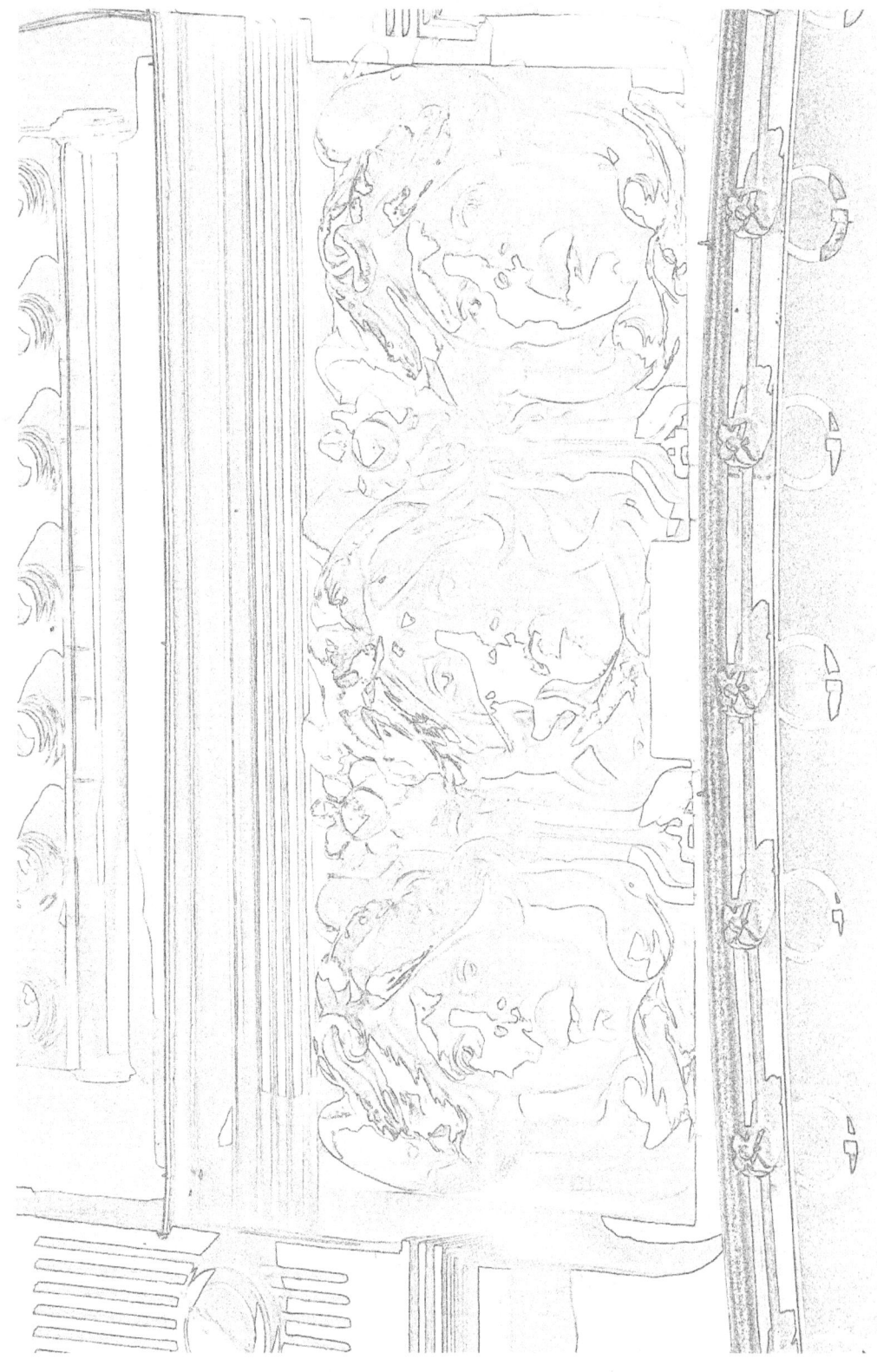

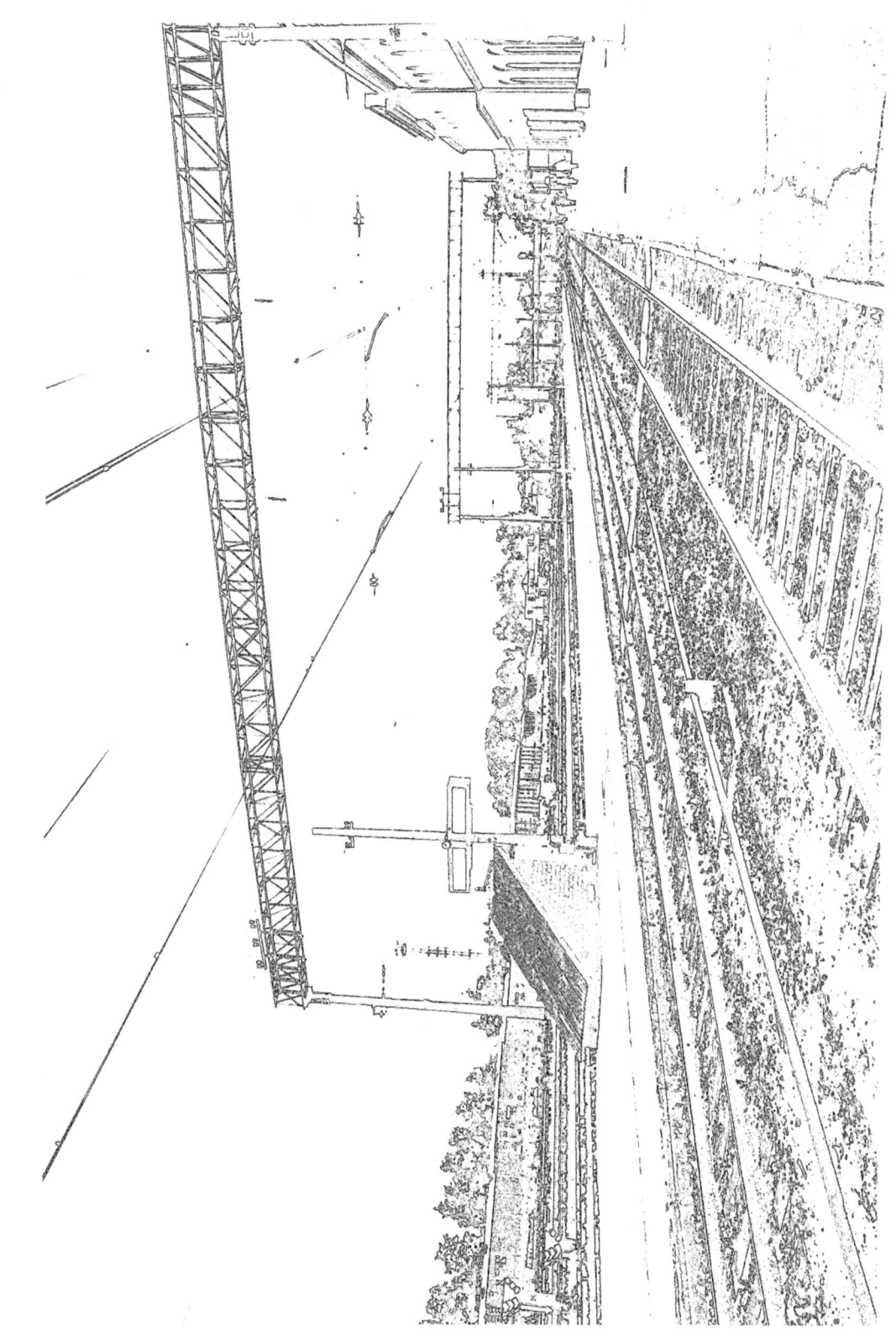

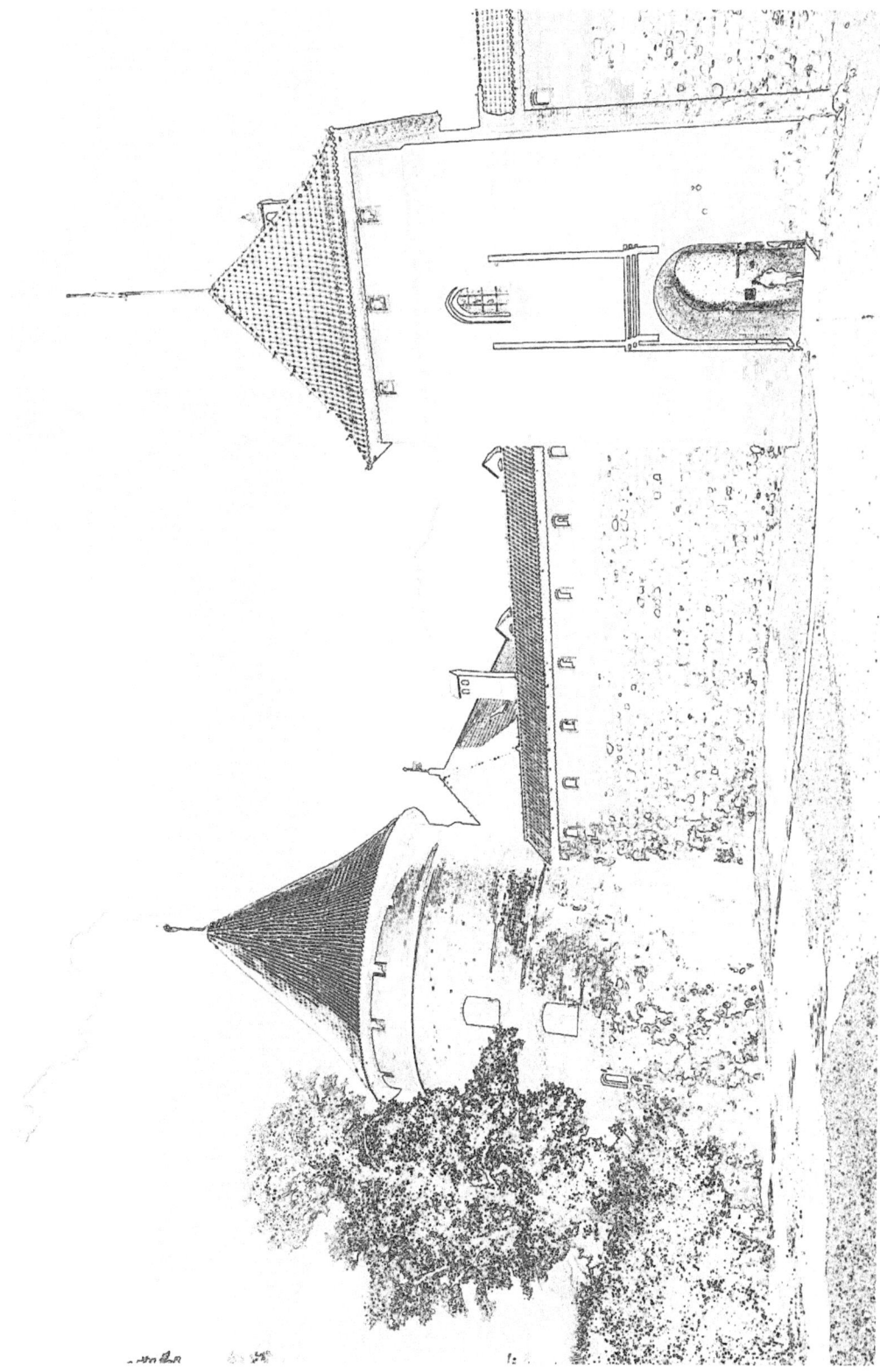

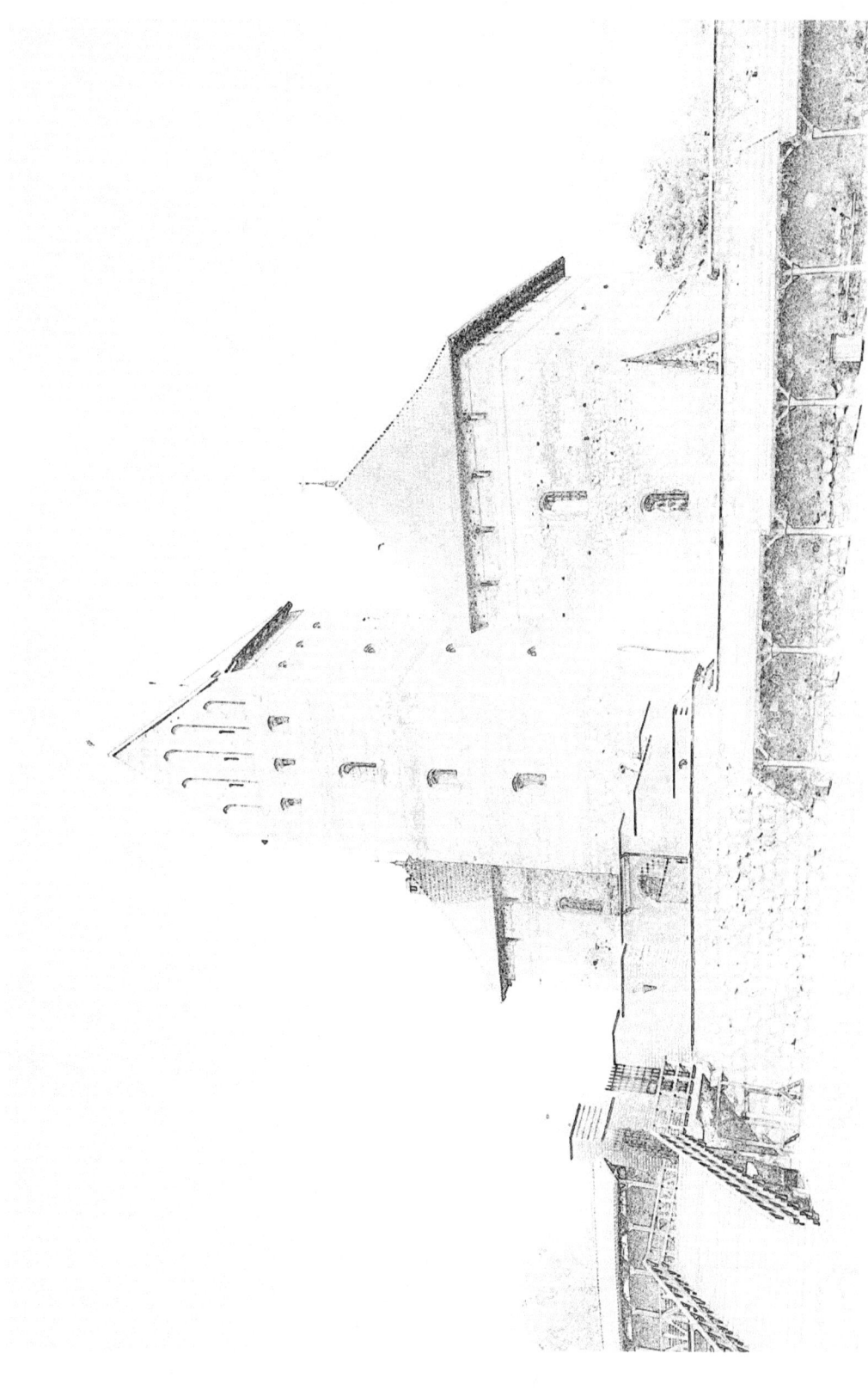

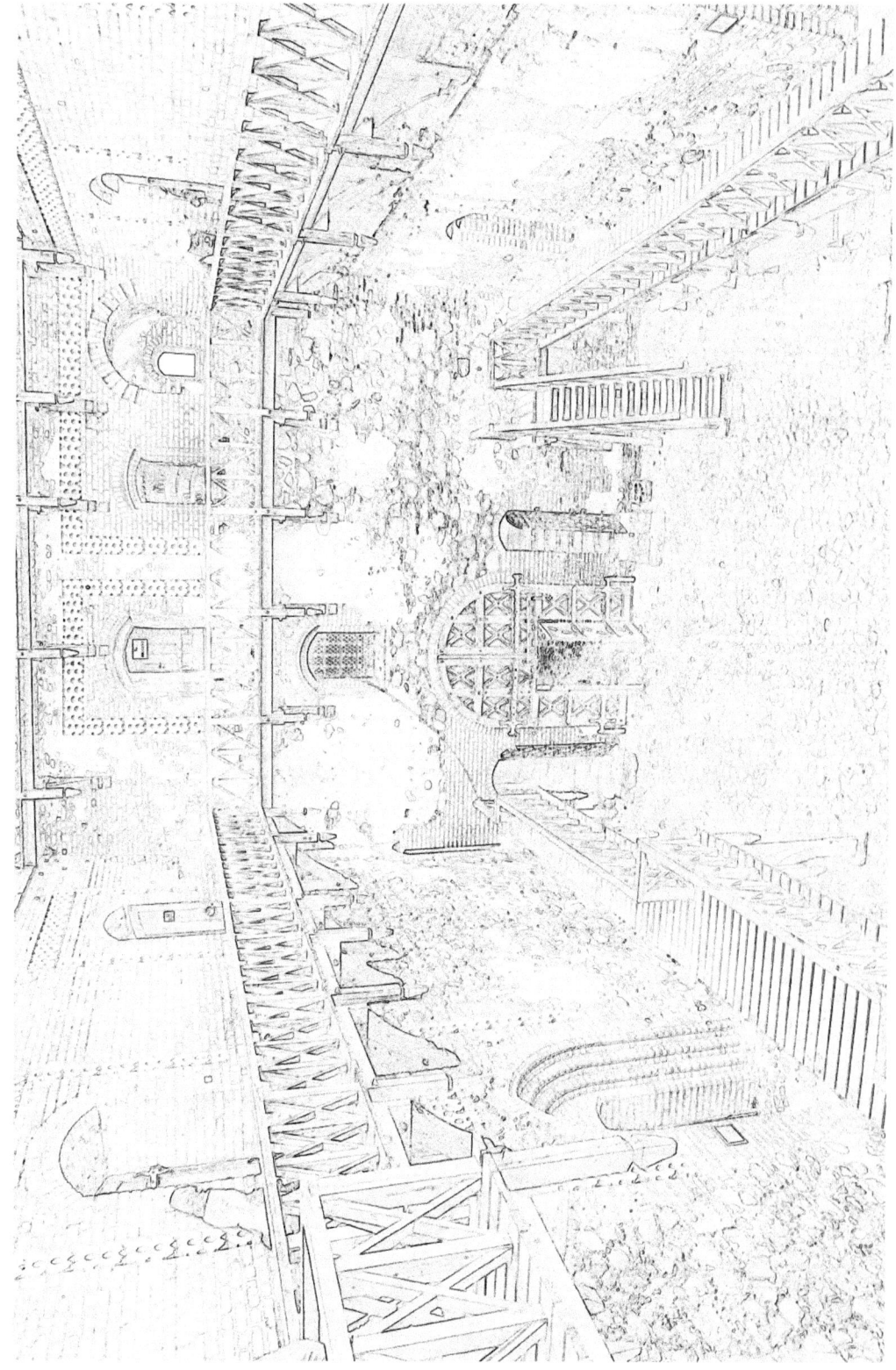

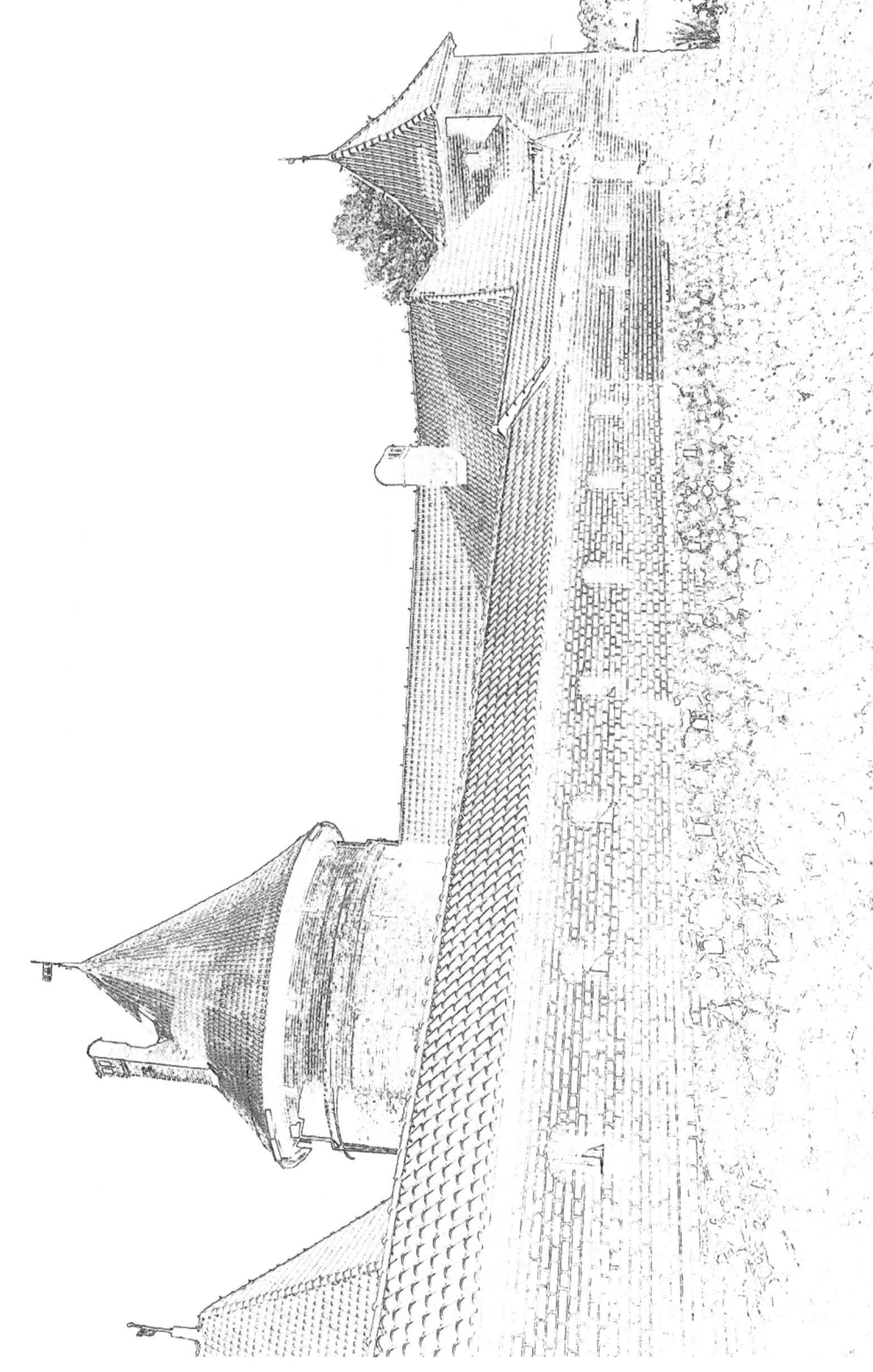

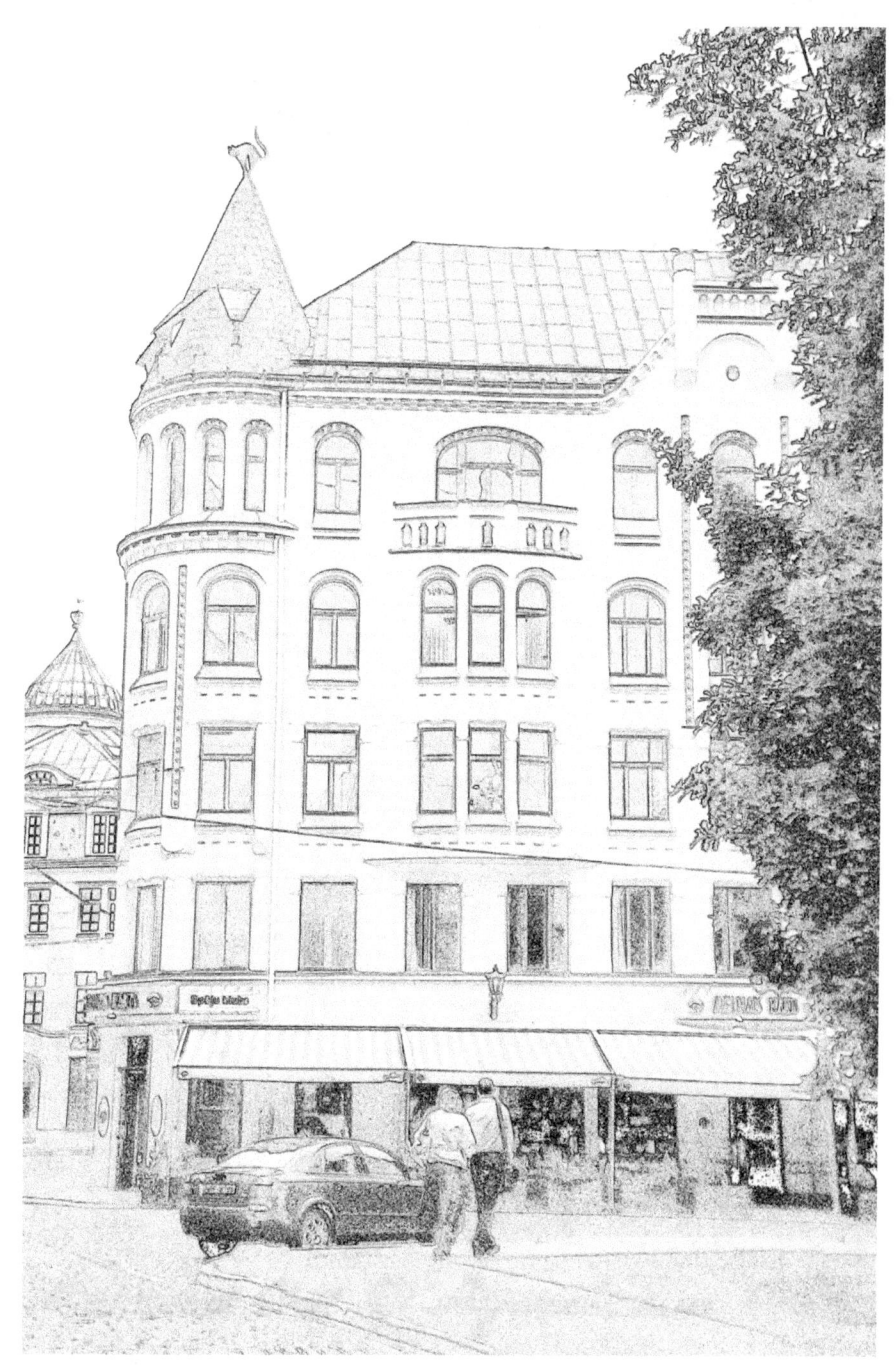

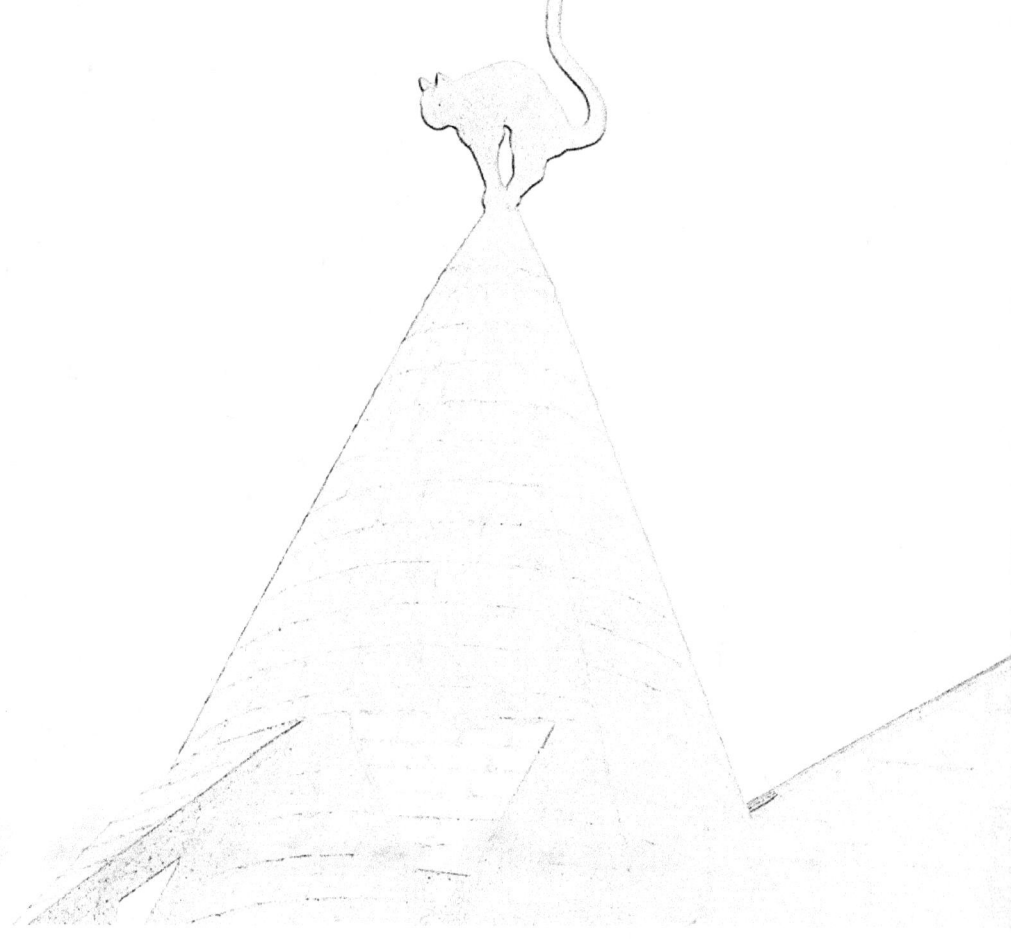

ABOUT THE AUTHOR

Born in Chesapeake, Virginia I acquired my human, Jack, on a sunny porch. A wonderful lady had brought me home, temporarily, after finding me outside a local mall. Jack learned about me, came over, and picked me up! We've been together ever since, adventuring, traveling, and enjoying fine food like dried squid and poke.

Please visit our webpage, AquinicumPress.com for free samples of upcoming work and links to other books from our publisher.

You can also sign up for email updates (no more than once a month) and additional free bonus materials.

I'd appreciate hearing your thoughts on the book, so we can make the next one even better. Please send me emails at **RelaxedCat@AquinicumPress.com**.

www.ingramcontent.com/pod-product-compliance
Lightning Source LLC
Chambersburg PA
CBHW081617170526
45166CB00009B/3011